MUSINGS

Alyssa Byrnes

Presentation by BookLeaf Publishing

Web: www.bookleafpub.com

E-mail: info@bookleafpub.com

ISBN: 9789358738865

First edition 2021

ACKNOWLEDGEMENTS

Thank you, Alvira Publishing, for this opportunity.

Thank you, Taylor Amy, for the front cover design.

Thank you, Mum, Dad, Bella, and Matt, for the constant support and inspiration.

Thank you, James, for every moment, memory, and the promises of future happenings that inspire my heart and mind every day.

For hopeless romantics and overthinkers.

1.   DAYDREAM

Snow settles on the windowsills

long before the sun rises,

perched perfectly beside the glass — good morning.

A glow settles on the mattress

long after the sun rises,

breaths between connected bodies — good morning.

Light settles on the breakfast table

long after the day's first words,

coffee, croissants and company — good morning.

Night settles on the wooden floor

long after the day's last words,

tucked in tightly together — goodnight.

2.   TIME FLIES

Little girls pick flowers from the garden,

and make potions out of dirt and fallen leaves,

knocked by the breeze,

playing games of witches

or horses

or fairies.

And they try to fly as they run,

around grass covered fields,

carrying a sword and shield,

through caves in their imagination

that make way

to glittering mermaid pools,

canopied by the tallest trees,

(almost as tall as dad).

Beneath their toes, the ground is soft,

covered in colourful mushrooms,

and moss.

They wash their bare feet

in flowing streams,

before returning home for

finger food and

fresh sheets,

and they keep pebbles on their bedside,

as day turns into night.

Before they sleep they speak to the moon,

with droopy eyelids

and wish on every star they can,

(that tomorrow is the same).

And they dream about their adventures.

3. SPILL

We would walk for hours to the riverbank,

and let the words pour from chapped lips,

dry mouths spilling over,

until our heads were almost empty,

and we finally reached the water.

There was always something more to come,

lasting little thoughts hiding at the edges,

and we wanted to fill the space,

force them out.

So we eased ourselves in.

Our bodies floated along the top,

spiders dancing across the surface tension,

achingly careful not to disturb the ripples,

as our final secrets dripped and dribbled

through our teeth.

We couldn't see far enough to watch as

the thoughts dragged slowly,

drifting down below our toes,

skin now wrinkled and mind freshly desperate,

for something else to chew.

So on we went once we were done,

searching for a new something past the trees

to fill the void that we had emptied.

And as always, we spared one final glance,

to thank the thoughts for leaving.

4.   862KM

I feel so

    f a r a w a y

And no matter

           how

                many

           steps

               I

                    take

the feeling stays the same.

But I suppose that's why they call it

     L

     O

     N

G

DISTANCE

7

5.   THE WAY WE SAY GOODBYE

The final kiss,

with the deep aching sadness we try to ignore,

like your bags that are packed and stacked by the door,

and the way that we stand there longing for more,

even though we know what we're doing this for.

The final touch,

with hands interlocked, no intention to move,

and no possible way for the tears to be soothed,

from the smiles that we force to contrast the mood,

to the way that our shoulders fall, now subdued.

The final glace,

with hiccupping breaths that catch in the throat,

the pit in my stomach that I hate the most,

as I watch the way that you grab your coat,

and I barely whisper; "please just don't go".

6. LOVE AT FIRST LIGHT

Hazy warmth broke on the horizon as Moon

chased the last few stars to bed,

she bid soft farewells on her departure,

as Sun finally rose his head.

And it was on that springtime morning,

sky full of pinks, becoming red,

that each waking bug and bloom

discovered Daisy to be dead.

They dared not reveal to Sun just yet,

as Mother Iris said;

"He will only suffer twice as much,

On a journey filled with dread".

And so they waited in the darkness

behind the garden shed,

gathered around the wilted child,

to weep for their lost friend.

A crowd had formed to mourn her,

as the warmth fell overhead,

and Iris turned to greet him first,

while all the others fled.

~

"Good morning Mother Iris.

How does your garden fare?"

She did not answer, leaves outstretched,

and eyes filled with despair.

Small buds watched from behind the trees,

whispering their silent prayer

as she took him round the garden path,

to witness the affair.

His eyes filled first with sorrow,

to see Daisy lying there,

parched and withered on cold bricks;

in the spot they used to share.

Sun crept along the stony trail,

time stopping as he stared

as he approached his sallow love;

the sight he almost could not bear.

He was rooted to the ground with her,

his heartache filled the air,

caressing her with anguished warmth,

for a love that was so rare.

7. THE BEST CUP OF TEA

A good cup of tea:

1. Fill the kettle (don't let the tap drip).

2. Set it on the stove and light the burner.

3. Make sure the lid is set over the spout.

4. Find your favourite cup.

5. Place the teabag in, wrapping the string twice around the handle.

6. Scream with the kettle once it boils.

7. Pour the boiling water.

8. Add milk (a dash or dollop to your liking).

The best cup of tea:

1. Ask mum to make you one
(she knows when to add the love).

8.   BEDTIME

Tonight is the kind of tired that hangs behind your eyes,

sitting heavy on your lashes to draw down your lids,

like bedroom blinds to block the setting sun.

It creeps up slowly,

then all at once, when you're

a little bit overwhelmed and maybe slightly weepy

from the weight of your shattered consciousness,

precarious on rigid shoulders

that crackle and pop when you stretch,

almost falling into rhythm with the ache beneath your skull

that has lasted all twelve hours of wakefulness.

On nights like these you forego the kitchen,

ignoring hunger cues and

haphazardly kicking shoes, scattered on your way upstairs

to the bed you made that morning,

thanking your past self for doing so as you

slither between the layers, cool cotton on your skin,

and body enveloped in the luxury that is the

promise of sleep.

It happens fast enough, lulled by the rain against your
window,

eyes closed without a second thought, and

mind drifting far and wide

before you can even think of counting sheep.

9.   WRITER'S BLOCK

Sometimes I just have nothing to say.

I put pen to paper,

or paper to pen,

and beg the words to leave my head,

but there are no words,

and there is no head,

and there is simply nothing.

Until there is,

and once there is

the words run off and taunt

from their hiding spot deep in the back

a lingering itch to scratch,

though sometimes I can't reach.

Eventually the ink flows,

and pages become littered with

ideas that aren't really full,

but at least they begin to be found,

and I can start with that,

until the first word meets the last.

10. GRANDPA

"Hi Dad, how are you today?"

He looked up at Mama, didn't know what to say.

"I brought the kids to say hello."

He didn't look like the man we used to know.

"Mum couldn't come, but let's give her a call."

He looked confused, but hugged us all.

"Here she is, I'll give you the phone."

I think he could tell that this wasn't home.

"Hello my darling, tell me how you're feeling."

He smiled at her voice, almost disbelieving.

"I heard you have some visitors for lunch?"

He looked over at us, eyebrows all scrunched.

"There's a woman here, and children too."

He spoke in whispers, not sure what to do.

"They seem very nice, she's helping me eat."

Mama set down his plate and brushed her cheek.

"I don't know them, why didn't you come?"

His voice was sad, Mama's head softly hung.

"I will come tomorrow, I promise it's true."

"And when you do, can I come home with you?"

"Maybe, my love. I'll always be here."

I looked over to Mama as she wiped her tears.

“Enjoy your meal, I’ll call back soon.”

He didn't want her to go, the one voice that he knew.

“I love you the most in this wonderful life.”

“I love you too, my beautiful wife.”

11. ADVENTURE HAT

A protector against the beating sun,

sitting atop a mess of hair,

privy to every story and song,

the Adventure Hat is always there.

The hat was fashioned in vintage shop,

edges rigid along the brim,

needing a journey to take new shape,

to add some character to the trim.

It holds up its duties in wet heat or dry,

crown shape collecting leaves and dew,

travelling with you, on roads far and wide,

never was there a companion so true.

It's one of those things that betters with time,

after years the best is yet to come,

so you can look back at all that has passed

and know your adventure has just begun.

One day it will sit on your bedroom wall,

displayed, with dust still deep in the seams,

to remind you of memories you may have forgotten,

of the old days spent living different dreams.

12. CATCHING MOONLIGHT

The harvest is a tricky time,

make sure your jars are clean and dry,

set up in neat and tidy lines,

for when the Moon at last will shine.

Don't forget to say the spell

so Moon knows that you wish her well,

(but whisper, there's no need to yell)

in hearing this, her heart will swell.

It's paramount to earn her trust,

for friends, she brings the gold stardust,

across the sky her light will brush,

when the eve has fallen hush.

Upon windowsills the magic sits,

to be captured when the daylight hits,

in each jar the night's enchantment fits,

one final, everlasting kiss.

13. LIFE LESSON

My parents really love each other,

but not in that

ooey,

gooey,

schmoopy way,

(though there's some of that too).

It's more like when life gets hard,

they choose to conquer

instead of crumble,

and better yet, they do so

hand in hand.

So growing up, they've taught me,

the greatest ways to

take a stand.

And I really love my partner,

with a healthy dose

of oo, and goo,

so I look forward to the battles,

life will throw our way,

because now that I'm grown,

I know exactly

what to do.

I don't like numbers anymore.

Or maybe it's that I don't really

trust them, because

every single time I put my faith

in kilograms or inches

I obsess over the way they behave,

always looking twice,

or too often,

so maybe it's me that I

don't really trust me,

but I'm trying.

And I do try,

to not fixate on the scale,

instead being driven by seeing new sights,

and hiking new heights,

stopping when I'm out of breath

instead of when

I've burned more numbers than I've consumed,

and I measure my waist

with simple twine,

and don't really focus on the length

of the line.

I hang it up behind

my bedroom door,

to revisit in maybe a month or more,

and I'm happy with that,

satisfied now with

everyday being made up

of three good meals,

and at least half an hour of sun

on my face,

focusing on the days ahead,

bursting with potential.

15. SUNKISSED BLISS

Tuck away the shells from the first trip,

store them in an empty jar

and whisper rhymes back to the ocean.

When you get home,

keep them on your bedside

so you can dream of moonlit tides.

Promise to visit often, and remember

hot sand on wet skin,

dry lips captured in a chaste kiss,

strands of salted hair

and pecks from the sun itself

left on bare, unprotected shoulders.

Soon enough the burn will fade,

and the tan will follow suit,

thereafter, all there is to do,

is cherish times gone by;

memories of the seaside.

31

16. FALLOUT

There's no escape from debris,

or the dust that settles

over everything in sight,

And there's nothing to do,

about crumbling walls,

with no one left inside

The wailing cries will fade,

into the distance,

following the setting sun.

In those darkening moments,

the howls begin to ring,

and the moon is yet to come.

The rolling night doesn't bring,

clarity or comfort

to hearts already broken,

The blow-up took place

inside the house,

none safe from the explosion.

17. PITTER PATTER

Rain splatters against

the frosted window panes,

slowly, surely,

drip

d

  r

   i

    p

dripping

'til it pools on the sill,

capturing the brief sparks of lighting;

becoming fairy lights along the wood panel

missed in a blink,

witnessed only by the droplets;

in awe of the finality of the bolt

punctuating the roar of the

cloud-covered sky.

18. CHANEL NO. 5

Mothers have a very particular way about them.

They know how to stay the same,

underneath whoever you need them to be.

My mother is a creature of habit,

and she always smells like flowers –

flowers and hairspray, and always like home.

I remember waking up on Saturday mornings,

being able to tell where she'd been,

following the scent that she left behind

as she padded about the house before work.

It started at her bedroom door,

leading to the kitchen where it swirled around

the aroma of freshly brewed coffee,

left behind for when Dad would wake,

before wafting towards the front door.

The wooden double doors didn't smell like anything,

unless it had been raining.

That's where I would lose the trail, but

she finished work at 6 o'clock,

and no matter what, she came home smiling,

smelling the same;

like mum.

19. FAKE FLOWERS

Fake flowers are just as nice as real ones;

the petals don't fall, and they make no mess,

there's no need to leave them out in the sun,

and in the long run they cost a lot less.

Take, for example, a wedding bouquet;

a lovely companion to take down the aisle,

your favourites to decorate your perfect day,

but in less than a week, those flowers will die.

And of course, there's the option to dry them out,

pressed between books for months on end,

that works very well, there is no doubt,

but if they break, what will you do then?

That's where we bring in polyester and wire,

made with such detail, you can hardly tell,

and truly, the only thing to provoke ire,

is the fact that the flowers are missing the smell!

20. DEATH?

Something comes at the end of things;

a final marker, sometimes

in the quiet moments,

after the beginnings and the journeys

and when there are no more in-betweens,

fading softly into silence.

Or maybe all too suddenly

long before the story should end

when there's still potential

and too many pages left to turn,

      - How could this be it?

Maybe it comes precisely;

exactly when it's supposed to,

punctuated with a final breath,

or one last line on the page,

- But surely there is more to come?

Beyond the ending, after

the last period, on

the last page, of

the last chapter.

Finality is the enemy of the soul,

"the end" is never

The End.